TESSA RANSFORD (www.wisdomfield.（ ... poet, translator, literary editor and cultu... acu.... ... . over the last forty years, having also worked as founder and director of the Scottish Poetry Library.

Tessa initiated the annual Callum Macdonald Memorial Award for publishers of pamphlet poetry in Scotland, now in its 14th year, with the attendant fairs and website: www.scottish-pamphlet-poetry. com. She has had Royal Literary Fund fellowships at the Centre for Human Ecology and Queen Margaret University. She was president of Scottish PEN from 2003 to 2006.

Tessa's *Not Just Moonshine, New and Selected Poems* was published in 2008 by Luath Press, and two books of poems have been published in 2012, also by Luath Press: *don't mention this to anyone*, poems relating to India and Pakistan, with Urdu calligraphy by Jila Peacock; and *Rug of a thousand colours*, a two-way translation book of poems based on the Five Pillars of Islam, with Palestinian poet Iyad Hayatleh, who lives in Glasgow.

MICHAEL KNOWLES is a portrait painter and photographer who has lived in Edinburgh since 1985.

He has paintings in the Scottish National Portrait Gallery, in other British public collections and in many private collections worldwide.

Made In Edinburgh

Poems and Evocations of Holyrood Park

TESSA RANSFORD

photography
Michael Knowles

Luath Press Limited
EDINBURGH
www.luath.co.uk

First published 2014

ISBN: 978-1-908373-84-7

The paper used in this book is recyclable. It is made from low chlorine pulps
produced in a low energy, low emissions manner from renewable forests.

The publishers acknowledge the support of

ALBA | CHRUTHACHAIL

towards the publication of this volume.

Printed and bound by Charlesworth Press, Wakefield

Typeset in 11 point Quadraat by 3btype.com

Contents

SUMMER

Acknowledgements

Some of the poems in this book first appeared in *Shadows from the Greater Hill*, Ramsay Head Press, 1987; *Edinburgh: An Intimate City*, Edinburgh City Council, 2000; *The Thing that Mattered Most*, a children's anthology, Scottish Poetry Library with Black and White Publishing, 2005; *Fras, Chapman* and *The Eildon Tree* magazines, *Not Just Moonshine*, 2008; and *Poems and Angels*, 2011.

Very many thanks are due to the photographer, my friend and neighbour, Michael Knowles and to Michael Lister, Roland Stiven, Sam Englebert, and staff at Luath for technical and editorial help.

Introduction

FOR THE LAST 30 years Arthur's Seat and Holyrood Park have been present as my immediate neighbours, always there for me outside my window in whatever mood or aspect they present themselves. That variety within stability is what nature gives us. I have responded with poems throughout the years and seasons.

From Ananda Coomeraswamy I learnt the concept of 'the transformation of nature in art'. But I came to realise that my relationship with Arthur's Seat is more a case of nature transforming my art. In darkness or light, winter or summer, the hill is 'stern and wild/meet nurse for a poetic child'. (This is how Sir Walter Scott describes Caledonia in The Lay of the Last Minstrel.)

Some of these poems have been published before, most notably in the book Shadows from the Greater Hill, Ramsay Head Press 1987, with photographs in black and white by the late Edwin Johnston. This time photography by Michael Knowles, and one who is constantly roving the hill with his camera, helps to show the dramatic contrasts and beautiful detail of the scene we share.

AD 142: the Romans in the Lothians

Once the spear of the Firth of Forth
What did the Romans seek?
Haar crept over the marshy land
where fast the rivulets flow
veins of crystal, pearl of the rock
Who commanded the heights?
from seven spurs of volcanic scaur
Castle, Corstorphine, Calton, the Crags,
Craiglockhart, Blackford and Braid?

Ditch and rampart the Antonine Wall
What did the Romans fear?
Tacitus knew that folk are enslaved
by bread and the circus lioness
as they forayed forth in marching blocks
to reconnoitre their practised path
to pacify and oppress.

A hard land, a wild land
What did the Romans know?
Deer and eagle and wolf and bear
cattle the counter of wealth and pride
princesses for royal heir
no single commander or emperor
but comrades who could fight and run
capture cattle and train the hawk
make sacrifice at the sacred rock
ensure the return of the year.

Night and day, dark and light
Why did the Romans go?
Winter or summer lives
no Roman rule could control the wind
or those ancient Scottish tribes.

WINTER

The hill and the park in winter are clear and cold. Black and white predominate. Moon and stars, the winter sun in frost, fog and snow, and fiery sunsets are a continual delight. Somehow the winter experience is almost secretly and personally ours. We live here.

Holyrood Park 5 November

faded colours, leaves on frosty grass
winter stillness, low-gleaming sun
a scarred and blackened hillside of burnt gorse

bonfire night and glinting fireworks
bangs and blazes people think are fun
faded colours, moon on frosty grass

dogs and ducks and all the little birds
tremble and take cover from the storm
of rockets lighting up the spiky gorse

on cliff ledges, towering rock face
above the ruined chapel standing firm
flaming colours, fierce on frosty grass

a night of fire: signal of the force
nature wreaks on any mere town
this blackened scarred hillside, burnt gorse

MADE IN EDINBURGH

27 November

'The moon doth shine as bright as day'
and that is no
childish exaggeration.

The night sky is blue in piercing moonlight
and overhead
at great height
the Hunter's moon has reached
a zenith
of light and cold and clear and star and
I sleep strangely
waking to morning's darkness.

TESSA RANSFORD

Holyrood Park at night

Snow and solo, Holyrood Park at night
flakes so brittle footsteps can press no print
    sky reflects the earthly pallor
        shadows of evening are blanched of darkness

Star nor moon, no break in the haze of white
outline none to sharpen the lion crag
    wide terrain of hill and parkland
        empty of creature beside my walking

Round the frozen loch sleep the ruffled swans
geese and lesser fowl in their sheltering
    dogs and humans huddle safely
        lights of the city for hibernation

Days are dark in winter and nights are pale
blankly folded into each other's sphere
    even gulls are muffled, humbled
        silently I alone travel forward

Far ahead I see by the gate the trees
hardened branches blurred by the pallid light
    nearly home I find beneath them
        circles of softness where earth is warmer

Friends grow distant lost in their own distress
each of us alone bears what winter brings
    stiffened frosted leafless upright
        yet unawares we make fonder patches

                                             MADE IN EDINBURGH

30 November

No bird can peck so thick a frost

Grass is hard, clod brittle

A thin dawn has thrown gulls
    from cliff edge
    tinged the sharp
mountain whose rock attacks the sky

Blackbird, thrush, push tamely
among dead leaves, scavengers

The parkland silent, silver

Among trees a piece whiter
    of soil
where frost nestled closer

Last leaves shall fall surely
yet they hang, cling with berries

I look clear, far
inhale with greed cold air

Moonlight over Arthur's Seat

Tonight the mountain has laid aside solidity:
    earth that has jutted and cragged its way into sky
with trapped molten intensities pushed to their utmost reach
    then cooled and folded, crumpled into shadows

Those massive columns now dissolve again in light
    wanly drawn about their huge shoulders
concentrated in an act of illumination
    with here and there a shaded boundary

Such exchange of substance noiselessly continues
    comprehends each separate, weightless leaf
each sweep of wilderness, each casual broken stone
    that shiningly betrays the eyes of gods

From their intimate gaze we seek a sheen of protection
    yet as they probe our levels of hidden light
we wager another moment towards our destiny
    and wrap ourselves in the sleep of our own courage

Seen and Scene

The mountain etched in white
stark trees and wing-born geese
the earth keeps quiet
below the snow and ice
but where some green appears
warmth has been exposed
and blessing seeps through
sealed by frost

Aeroplanes at Night

The aeroplanes flew over in darkest space
their roar was louder heard in the hush of night
    lit up in starry outline like a
        skeleton, luminous, heading westward

They keep formation, each one above the next
direction, speed, together in perfect time
    but only light-shape, trav'lling sound-stream
        sensible, all the construction hidden

A pattern lit by love as it shows me up
is all that can be seen of my voyaging
    when tedious body weight and daily
        selfhood is lost in surrounding darkness

And you, who fly with me, alongside but high
above the earth to destiny ever dark
    the keeping course our only order
        light answers light, nor do engines falter

Trees in winter sunlight

Leaning pale against the hill
in this long Lenten fast
tall trunks intangible
cast shadows on the slope
sinister, substantial

Shadow
more real
than substance
and the cause of this reversal:
winter

Half-hearted sun
casts a twitch of smile
across the woods
where frost unmelted
seals the sap

Leaning pale
against the hill
all my substance gone
heavy, sinister,
sloping, shadowy
into this hard ground,
forced
into a season of austerity

12 December

Geese now feed among the gulls
glad of meadow grass
when once they spanned the northern wilderness

The darkening sky is darkened by
their multitudinous flight
as around the hill they uttering wheel

A spaniel ran among them as
they fed, and they have risen
as one, alight, and feed again in flock

Gulls, too, are circling
noisily by the window
as if there were agreement in dissent

Celtic heads and beaks and knotted
necks with vivid eyes
have come to life around me

Jackdaws

black daws
Jackdaws

hill daws
Jilldaws

who knows
hips and haws

something dead
flowerbed

food and water
wind shelter

bark and berries
cherries

cat claws
dog gnaws

silver birch
safe perch

jackpair
in the air

jackwife
jackknife

little chat
this and that

latest trends
jack friends

MADE IN EDINBURGH

TESSA RANSFORD

24 December

There is a theory that 'Apollo' denotes a set of concepts and ideas in music, astronomy, geometry and mathematics which was widespread in the megalithic era, linked to the Druids and later to the Pythagoreans. The story goes that 'Apollo' left the shrine at Delphi in the winter months to *dwell among the Hyperboreans*. A suggested explanation is that the two constellations, the Lyre and the Swan, associated with Apollo, were more visible in that era in northern lands in winter.

Apollo winters here;
strings his lyre like stars
through clouds, like swans
brightened in the wind;
practises his geometries
scaled to our particulars,
arcs, crags, promontories.

A coiled, constricted formula
translated into sections of our landscape,
our city-weathered hill;
reduced yet refined
from Delphic drama, grandeur
or golden Minoan harmony;
his circles here, triangles,
his proportions are coded
into our alpha rock,
our liquid sky, diagonal,
and huge, cold, omega winter nights.

Song for snow

Golden leaf on silver bough – break
Branches under snow – shake
A Siberian wind – flakes
Drift deep below

Black cloud thunder mass – glow
Of midday outline – through
To the gleam and glimpse – blue
Shadows on the hill

Dark and light together – spill
With birds raucous as they – fill
The glen and loch and – will
Skein their way south

Winter now forms our world – north
Spin the seasons – earth
Works her systems – death
with birth interdwelt

Glaciers may return or – melt
Ice or flood our future – dealt
All beneath Orion – held
As we marvel faithfully

A watercolour poem

A watercolour poem to be held
for opening only in the weakest light
a poem of resilience and routine,
the dimmer kind, accepting, reticent
not set to prove itself, fight some good fight
but oblivious to its own design
not noticeable even, noticing
likeness, oddness, traces lingering

The muddy pathway purified in snow
and hillside magnified in frosty sky
that full moon, thirteenth in the year,
on Ne'er Day, ominous, unusual, blue
widefarer, presageful, to clarify
the watercolour faith that thaws our fear

1 January – time made new

We have crossed the threshold
into time made new.
We make it new by stepping
bravely from the familiar
to proceed into a circle
narrower but higher
bearing with us
what we can
all that ringed us what we are
but opening this horizon
in each other
for our neighbour
by the truth of our endeavour.

5 January – Turner watercolours

As daylight dims the stars
so consciousness is wakeful over dreams.

Turner's watercolours
are not exposed to view
except in Scotland's
month of darkness
when no strong light destroys them.

Winter discovers
what summer hides:
dreams, ancient magic,
fragile water-colour feelings.

Waxwings in the Park

A flock of waxwings in the sycamore
sycamore in February in the park
park green and windswept in the city
city grey yet glistening in the east
east coast of Scotland facing Europe
Europe, Scandinavia and Siberia
Siberia which sends its icy greetings
icy greetings holding back the Spring
Spring to come, longer light and walks
walks in the park perhaps to glimpse
crested waxwings banded on the boughs

In Scotland *occasional winter visitors*
visitors who wear distinctive colours
colourful from head to yellow tail
yellow tail and sealing-wax red tip
to every feather of the wings, wings
for chasing insects, beaks for berries
beret chestnut with the jaunty crest
pinstriped through in charcoal black
and black around the throat and blazing eye

My eye surprises me in looking up
looking up and welcoming the migrants
migrants among our crows and starlings
our gulls accustomed to the slanting sun

1 February

Snow
the loch white
and black, where birds drink:
geese, swans, ducks, golden eye and moorhens,
coots, gulls, pigeons
walk on snowy ice.

The water has no edge.

Toboggans churn the milky snow
with slaps of laughter, shouts,
dogs, kids,
creaming the afternoon
in blinding sun, deafening speed.

A puppy is carried;
toddlers cling to mothers on the sledge
who bump and swerve and fall and go again
like girls, like children.

Cars wait while geese cross the road
cackling but unhurried;
they circumfly the hill, the houses and the road
and land again where water used to be;
they sit heavy-breasted in the snow
and dab thirsty beaks.

SPRING

Cherry blossom and gorse make silver and gold blazoning the hillside. The wagtail returns and crosses our path, while birds are nesting, new leaves appear and the equinox brings longer light, sun, and showers, but snow can still return. It is time to be out and up and in tune with the hill as it awakens from its winter quiet.

9 March

The geese have gone.

I saw them
walking under the trees
not feeding, walking,
and wondering if it was time.

They must have judged
that day was equal to night,
warm was level with cold,
the loch now too small
for fledged ambition.

The geese have gone.

No-one saw them leave.

They did not think, they flew
and somewhere in the guts of a gale
they are winging
heavy body steady
beak pointing ahead

as they cry into the wind
and keep formation
at last to sink again
by some wide stretch of melting lake,
their undebated, undesired
yet undoubted destination.

29 March

Knee-deep in snow,
dark, wet, cold scentlessness,
old tall trees
are striped white to windward.

Those young trees
have no roughnesses
for catching flakes
to build a thin streak
of snow-shading.

In a blizzard
none can run away that is rooted.
The wind does not relent,
drives cold in sideways,
etches black and white.

Equinox

the dark days are done as we turn towards light
white on black like swans on water and the jaunty pied wagtail appears
in black and white with the first daisies in flower in the long grass wet
with haar while the kestrel hovers above a single dandelion and
a cloud of almond blossom conceals the singing robin

March weather

Wind in pines
wind on water
wind in rushes
wind on feather

Sun in leaves
sun on loch
sun in reeds
sun on duck

Rain in trees
rain on river
rain in moss
rain on Eider

All one morning
all together
in an hour
March weather

Observation of mating toads

Uxorius toad
on road
through wood
you could
be stone
dark brown

walk nearer
see clearer
you stop
bufo flop
down cower
yet lower

loaded pack
natterjack
not alone
not one
another creature
double decker

half your size
sprawled lengthwise
as if dead
your newly-wed
puny husband
moribund

we've passed
take a last
look at you
one and two
now you crawl
quite a haul

on the verge
you merge
in mud
with your stud
will you greet him
will you eat him?

Spring walk

Close up bluebells almost assault the eye
yet spread through the woods they shimmer as mist

Sunlight settles on primroses
and shade sits with violets
beside the reedy pond

Mossy stumps are starred with anemones
and ferns uncurl their music

Silvery leaves emerge from massive branches

while all of a sudden
half-hidden
a floating raft of cowslips

the birds are enraptured
and recklessly sing in chorus

5 April

I glimpsed that red moon setting on Good Friday morning
6am directly face to face.
It sank behind the ridge without delay
in the corner of my just-opened eye.

It was burnished by what must have been the sun
rising, but I was too asleep to rise and
look towards the east. I let the moon slip
and myself slumber, in that early glow.

Easter Day

Darkness before dawn
and rain
rhythmical
encompassing within its sound
ourselves, the window ledges,
street and buildings,
cars, trees, grass, gate, wall.

It washes clean the mind
and cradles agitation.

We enter the temple of listening
where arabesque of birdsong
decorates the dawn
above the drumming peace,
the steady lethargy,
even the dull blessedness
of rain.

13 April

Rain diagonal
screens the mountain flank
in April, in daylight,
in sharp, clear stripes
against brown grasses
of a winter coat unmoulted,
except in muddy patches
where, long and damp,
it greens and thickens.

16 April – transplanted

Trees do not grow for three or four years
after being transplanted;
they settle their roots.

These trees in the park
are large to have been uprooted.
The younger the tree
the quicker it settles and grows;
so I am told.

My experience is different:
roots were dragging me under.
I could not grow for the heavy clinging.

Transplanted now
I am lifted, winging
weightless almost.

My growing is to shed
all that holds me down.

I grow stems of thought
to flower as poems.

25 April

The chapel ruin is in shade
on its level,
sheltered from the east wind
and rising sun.

The remnant wall faces north.

Window-gaps, like eyes,
still survey the centuries
and look at us
from every quarter.
They stare in shadow
or fill with quickening light.

I return the gaze
saying
'Yes, I soon shall pass,
while you remain.'

Yet traces of my abiding
may appear, with apertures
that take in sky and mountain.

Cygnets on Dunsapie

A cold Spring and damp start to summer
but the flowers are not downcast:
vetches, ladies' smock, birds-foot
trefoil and bloody geraniums
sparkle forth their purples and
whites in mist and cloud.

Gorse and broom are fading
as laburnum and lilac appear;
ducklings scootle along at the edge
of the loch while an ungainly
coot chick stands dumbly on a stone.

A heron ignores the cars and children,
squalling gulls and persistent crows
to gobble slithers of this and that
snatched from the water.

But today another story:
five pale grey cygnets
black-eyed and slender necked
ploiter in the long grass
enveloped by their parents

whose large beaks and folded wings
whose lissom looping necks
are bent above around them
solicitous and yet unfussing.

Week after the week the cob and pen
took turns
to sit on their huge white eggs
in rain and wind, dark and light,
occasional sun or moon,
hungry and cold but unflinchingly
patient.

Now among their brood
they are oblivious to all else
in reverence for this life, this present moment
and this expected strangeness.

TESSA RANSFORD

59

Edinburgh, April evening

Herring gull on a chimney pot
above and around crosses, crowns,
corbelling, even a sphinx;
clock strikes from St Giles
in a sky of delicate clouds
as shadows revolve
on dome, cupola, stone
of Edinburgh's Old Town.

Aeroplane silvers across
above and around gull-nested crags
and the spikey new parliament.
A crude red lion with blue claws
on the Queen's Gallery
not rampant except for commerce –
has no roar for the politicians.

By Canongate Kirk the poet is walking
in sculpture, Robert Fergusson,
before his fall and desolate death.
He clutches his youthful poems which
berate the wily lawyers and praise
'the braid cloth' of plain speaking in Scots.
Above him cherry trees bow, and bless
that inner life of literature, unmanageable and alive.

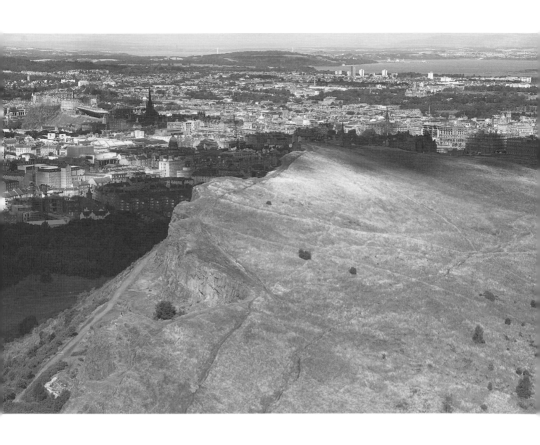

Homeseeker

Thirty miles an hour for ten hours a day
swallows fly home to the place they nested in
last year, where they were hatched themselves.

They do not take the chance of warmer southern summers
passing through Spain and France
and England on their way to Scottish glebes.

Swallows will change their nest only when destroyed.

My home is equally in my head and I seek it
always, not allowing myself to rest.

The silver birch shimmers in pale leaves.
I think of her as a daughter far away,
the beech and ash her sisters.
My son is the pine tree strong and tall.

Like the swallows though he will leave, making
winter for me. I tell myself to stay
and fill today with calm, brooding love.

The patient river speaks. Trees and birds
that remain throughout the year surround me nestfully.
Contentment is a duty, the home I seek.

SUMMER

The beauties of summer are more subdued, green on green. Cygnets and ducklings swim on the lochs. The yellow broom and trees in leaf give a luxurious heady sense of exhilaration. People are everywhere now, not just the runners and dog-walkers but kite-flyers, cyclists, picnickers and groups training for football, or enjoying rounders and cricket. At weekends there are often major events, races and marathons. The grasscutter loops from end to end of the park cutting swathes of grass to cling to our shoes in reminder of who is in control.

The swifts swoop high and low, while large young gulls and crows demand attention from the patient parents. The hill in summer is host to files of people by day and night and it hears everyone's secrets and all the world's languages.

1 May

Today, the first of May
the sun was seen to rise
over contradictory cloud
at 5.30 in colour

and young girls attended
silent
who had climbed the hill chattering

As the orb achieved wholeness
they broke into dancing, singing
and running downhill to breakfast

5 May

To combine hard, dark, enduring substance
with here-today-gone-tomorrow blossom
within repeated cycle of foliage:
that is the fascination
(now I see it)
that is the satisfaction
in a tree.

Now I know why we worship them.
We see in them
our own toughness
and our weak extremities,
our own endurance and ephemera.

Young cherries stand in scant flower
calm in quiet roundels.

They chide me
not to look away
not to look with disillusion.
They demand humility
a self-forgiving smile.

7 May

The hill is hiding its head day after day
and even at night
a strange indigo aura covers the peak.

The sun has not been seen
no more has the moon
in all this milky seedtime.

Gulls can hardly fly for weight of cloud.

Trees succumb to gravity
and people with grey resentments
sway and droop.

After so many days, to witness
the head of the mountain clear
its thoughts in order,
is revelation, an outline of truth.

20 May

Summer makes the world soft
adds texture to birdsong

The mountain gently nuzzles the sky

Grass and trees conjoin
horizontal with vertical

Insubstantial as shadow
the propped frame
of the ruined chapel

Summer waives outlines
merges soft on softness...

Day of Summer

A day of summer came to the city

We couldn't be sure to begin with
like snails putting out our horns
but then we decided to risk it without a raincoat

Foreign students from the language schools
kept on their cardies and fleeces

Lawyers were still in suits
Adam Smith on his new pedestal
was buttoned in coat and whig
but lily-white Scottish lads began
to take off their shirts and
sit on steps and others
dashed into shops to buy a top
that allowed their shoulders and upper arms
to be touched by sun
at last
    And so it came to pass
    on that day of summer
    in Edinburgh

Falling Shadows

Grass is flaunting its green after snow,
men with kites, women with dogs,
parents with bikes, scooters, buggies
and higher where clusters and couples
are climbing, delighting.

View and breath:
below the kites and then
how their shadows glide black
on the bright, concealing
their strings. A bird's
winged shadow – only
a gull. Then another, black,
flutters down. No shadow, a crow,
but its shadow is croaking.

Over the ridge the familiar city,
its old and new faces.
Fulmars are courting beneath the crag
on ledges of rock that for years
have been in danger of falling.
Beware. I stumble and then recover.
Long, emaciated, my shadow stretches.

The moon, half grown and white
is still on a string up there.
What falls or befalls, what casualty,
what case can be made, what fate,
how fell, how fallen?

Descend to the parents' level again
to the children, their little voices,
as an aeroplane in shining armour
traces its circling route
striking its shadow through us.

MADE IN EDINBURGH

28 May

Swifts spring from air
from nowhere
born of new light

They exist in air, on air
follow the windstream from country to country
crossing turbulent oceans

Seekers of longer light, wider space,
they skim the loch where swans shine
as waters darken and overturn,
trees sway low

Do swifts believe in night?
They don't believe they imagine
they imagine life is a dance

space and light the music
darkness only the prelude
to more ethereal melodies

20 June

The actual moment when
early in the haze of day
a quality appears of incandescence

the whole world whitens
hill slides slowly out of mist
swells towards intrusion of light

I am invaded by that moment:
no annunciation
but epiphany; treasures

brought from history, humanity
like golden weapons salvaged
from beneath the seas

Dark night, soul's night
my night enduring
silence of the dark broken
dawn-dove returning

First light, day-light
my light assuming
waited-for word spoken
tongues of flame burning

Day in the park

we play in the park
the gulls the geese and labradors

my friend is training a pack of puppies
school parties are picnicking
air and earth sparkle with light

I walk through the park
the labradors the gulls and geese

people run, fly kites, play rounders
the mower cuts the grass in circles
all length and breadth of the afternoon

I wait in the park
the geese the labradors and gulls

now few remain as clouds amass

and one by one they all go home

as gusts of wind collapse the grass

1 July

Shadows from the greater hill
in early eastern light, project
upon the lesser slope, to fill
with dark its curves and hollowings –
as suddenly, without remark,
white gulls open huge black wings.

10 July

A great dane is strolling in the park.
He lopes
left feet together
then right.

His head is high.
He feels in proportion
to the mountain.

Young trees fluster
inches above him.

His flanks are moving
in a strathspey.

His paces are longer
then those of his companion
who trips in jeans
and white, heeled shoes.

He keeps his distance
unable, quite, to own her.

11 July – *tête-à-tête*

Just where they fell
sprawled in the park
on sunlit grass
a bike, a boy, a girl
in black, white and steel

It is evening
they do not move for an hour

their shadows move

The boy and girl converse
heads together, feet apart

The bicycle is silent

Summer

golden
birds
dawn
rocks
moon
lapped
tide
trapped
touch
night
sleep
light
barley
field
starry
world

Silver and Black

black water

black rocks

black trees

black sky

black grass

silver rocks

silver trees

silver sky

silver grass

silver water

black heart

black tongue

black eyes

black hair

black nails

silver tongue

silver eyes

silver hair

silver nails

silver heart

black soil

black claws

black bird

black berry

black leaf

silver claws

silver bird

silver berry

silver leaf

silver soil

black death

black life

black night

black day

black time

silver life

silver night

silver day

silver time

silver death

MADE IN EDINBURGH

Dragonfly

dragonfly
heaven's spy
    beckoner
    eye-catcher
follower
agitator
    devil's needle
    angel's spindle
slender legged
upper lipped
    double wings
        up in a whirr
shimmerings
now where
    threadbare
    pine and fir
the waterfall
dare or die
    tells it all
    dragonfly

1 August

After the rains
gulls are fishing the grass
for worms.

They ripple over the surface
breasting the sunlight
and follow curves of the mower
where it circled the island of trees.

Worms are rising out of flooded tunnels.

It's easy fishing:
no need to scream and dive.

The hill is green and juicy;
it's never known so much moisture,
unaccustomed to luxury.

I'll paddle over the grass again
and catch medieval mushrooms
on an ancient duelling-ground.

3 August – dawn winds

The hill is tossing high frail wisps of
rosy cloud to glide in steady gale
along a turquoise sky around above the
perpendicular and slightly askew columns
above the triangular gap
between crown and crag.

The moon full at midnight
is now high and faded
almost a lazy eyelid
day's eye opening
or night's eye closing.

Birds chase and ride the wind
reeling wheeling
aware that in a moment
ordinary flight of day will have to be resumed.

The hawk alone is steady
keeps position despite the gale
to pinpoint a victim

and far below
grasses tinge in flower:
harebell, yarrow, lady's yellow bedstraw
among the rangy thistles and fatted doves.

Skipping over the hill

*The mandrakes gave forth fragrance, and at our doors are all
manner of precious fruits, new and old, which I have laid up for
thee, O my beloved.*

Song of Solomon 7:14

When I heard you were coming
I pictured you skipping over the hill
with a roll on your skateboard
a tumble and spill

I didn't have milk
I hadn't even a loaf of bread
no presents or goodies
nor had I made the bed

Your favourite pudding –
I looked for where I had hidden the sweets –
scented only the mandrake root
of my poems and books

what have I stored for you
new and exciting since your last visit?
The CD you wanted
a note for your wallet

and I have uncovered
the cowrie shells you once stooped and collected
a little chap, one long afternoon
on the beach at North Berwick

I've safekept them for you
in a precious embroidered treasure bundle
at the back of a drawer
in the bedside table

O my beloved
I give you my unsparing love and my art
and laying up of your days in
the memory cupboards of my heart

4 August

The night sky is like a Gauguin girl:
dusky and gorgeous.

The ancient chapel stands
narrow, gaunt,
inclined on its headland
like a bard or prophet
who would be harkened to.

I met the moon at eye-level
easterly and grainy
raising its amplitude
above the lower slopes.

Touchstone

warm
cold
quick
dead
crone
bride
the arch priestess

sharp
pleated
sloped
straight
strong
grounded
the ruler upright

sea
shore
cave
contour
high
low
the far alignment

awake for spring
dawn and colour
for sun and moon
long wake of winter

wheel of shadows
weave of stars
and eyelids close
at crimsoned dusk

11 August

After dark, light
after dawn, grey
after wind, calm
after rain, dry

A tiny white terrier scampers among the gulls
a black speck of kestrel hovers among the clouds

Beside the loch, trees are weary with their leaves
young trees, established, begin to lean slightly
a jogger runs in red with bare white legs
as if from a tree-top I accept the scene
given each morning
calm, grey light

I want no sudden sun
no burst of rain or wind
this peace, this unemphatic
non-expectant, poised
detachment
I have worked for

Gorse Girl

My gorse girl
dazzling pale
quine o' the whin
scorns to smile

Gold effulgence
brutal thorns
the suffering
that builds a crown

From your nature –
delicate, sharp,
sheer, enduring –
no escape

It will keep you
growing wild
in wind and sun
in rain and cold

You will make
your scented flowers
appear again
they will resurge

In bold abundance
to brand the hill
with spreading brilliance
fiery girl

MADE IN EDINBURGH

Ambience

Smoke, like mist, is drifting round the hill
dense and stench the summit invisible

blackthorn and whin that spread like fire themselves
are flaming now in fire along the slope

rabbits will have scuttled underground
beetles too will burrow safely down

what of the singing thrush I stopped to see
and where the yellow-hammer, and their nests?

today the clouds are only clouds and
cool winds soothe the black scars on the hill

rock and earth will benefit from ash
and new shoots will know nothing of the past

song, flower, stir and hope of life
precariously suspend on rock and cliff

Sun on Bass Rock
(as seen from Arthur's Seat)

rain cloudiness
sunset gleam
indigo sea
one silver ray
a sudden diamond
gannets stream
halo radiant
in the moment's beam

AUTUMN

Walking through the park and up the hill in Autumn is the most delightful of all. Rowanberries shine, with hips and haws and brambles, while leaves turn brown and red and gold. The robin sings in the same place each day so that mind and strength are restored and stored against winter.

13 September

swifts are dashing into the wind the wild west wind and in
   streams of sun
they cry as they fly 'goodbye goodbye; this our last day; see you
   next May'
and gulls and geese are drying their feathers sedately patching
   the green of the grass and they watch the swifts in their whirl
   and whisk
and they sigh and nod and continue to stand and stalk and stake
   their claims to the park
red leaves for me and winter's breath, the mist on the hill,
   shrouded, still

23 September

The loch has overflowed its banks.
The moon is overripe with juice.

Ducks were fed from this submerged pavement
and that lagoon was formerly the grass.

Water is taking to the road
and downhill to the traffic-lights.
What use are wheels?

Yet summer boats have gone
and swans return
with six enormous cygnets
to this enlarged domain.

One inch of rain
has altered our boundaries.

6 October

Tree in full leaf
wind in full blow
sun in full shine
make a shadow
that dances
dances.

Summer has gone
grass has grown
sky is clean
and darkly
the shadow-tree
dances.

Is this how Orpheus made trees move,
sun and wind his aid?

I applaud, and record
exactly this will never happen again:

I must hold them together
light and shade
wind and sun
grass and tree
impossibly dancing shadow.

13 October

swifts have flown over the hill and far away
sunlight tries to stay strong and is weaker each day
for as the earth turned at the equinox I too was reversed
and now walk step by stealth breathing in and out
and chant my way into winter

14 October

I know the time of year and how trees
are experiencing these first loving
touches of newly-awakened frost
which quietens autumnal trembling.
Beside the loch they are yellow
except for the willow,
but young trees in their roundels
are wispy and frail.
It takes a mass of withered leaves
for abundant colour.

The mower perhaps is working one last time
to leave the grass evenly smoothed
before the churning of winter.
Swifts have gone, but geese
flock and fly and land and walk and swim.
They own the place in their noisy way.
Birds are scarcely singing now
but berries are brilliant;
even beside the bus-stop on the roadside
haws are darkly bloody.
Rowans are dotted with crimson
as if welcoming winter:
its clear, piercing, crying, enduring love.

Going for the paper

I walk the same path
place my feet like a tiger
breathe the same count

Robin sits on the same twig
sings the same song
keeps the same rhythm

He sings out loud
I respond in my heart

Embroglio

This body a carapace
shell for molluscs of thought
a pack of gregarious senses
of inaudible resonances
happy loving hurt

As we join the circus of life
intelligent cells coalesce
encounter the earth minutely
while part of the planet completely –
survival the quiet test

Plants, such givers of life
seeds, a prism of colours
sharers and makers of water
of feelers of roots of rapture
and soundless orators

To wait is the hardest demand
on the human unsatisfied mind
on the human impatient heart
whose senses are truly refined
when dark deaf silent and blind

Seeings

Suddenly an apple tree
beside the path up to the crags
fruit abundant, untouched,
each one half green, half rosy
in the sun.

In the dell
grows a russet-stemmed poplar
with olive green leaves,
and a scrawl of ripe brambles.

On the slope
a fairy ring of purple daisies,
daystars for Michaelmas.

Fruit, tree, flowers
unspoilt, unpicked, unbroken.

Soon the harvest moon will float
above them, quietly there.

8 November

In single file beside the loch
they fade, the trees, they tinge,
they do not shed their leaves
but manifest their branches.

How calm and green the scene:
it is as if
all manner of thing shall be green
and all shall be green
and certainly small is behovely.

I am framed by my window frame
waking to white flutter of gulls,
scruffy, friendly hump
of the multi-verdant mountain.

St Francis would have felt at home,
respectfully addressed it as 'big brother'?

17 November

The sun at its zenith
is level with my windows

It makes pale with pleasure
the park
and the last topmost
yellow leaves

Young trees have shadows
like spokes
pointed due north towards me

With massive stillness
the mountain hovers in shade

Never in summer was this suspension:
a bird moves
and silhouetted verticals
of tiny people climbing the mountain

A cloud moves
when steadily watched

Autumn sunlight

If wet leaves turn to silver
and dry leaves turn to gold
what need of further alchemy
from commerce or academy
or metals bought and sold?
The elixir is in our eyes
which makes this world a paradise

FULL CIRCLE

We have completed the cycle of the seasons and understand that the land is both physical and metaphysical. Drovers marked out paths through the hills and glens and over the rivers; and centuries before them druids and pilgrims walked from one holy place of learning to another. The dragons of pre-historic myth and legend can be understood in terms of the climate change challenges facing us now, and Merlin is forever returning to guide us in unexpected ways.

Drovers

Take three onions a handful of oatmeal
ewe's milk and ox blood
a bannock or two
ram's horn of whisky

Black pudding and porridge for men and dogs
stirred with cold water if no chance of fuel

Coarse brown plaid homespun checker
reeking of peatsmoke bracken and heather
thick-coated hirsute bearded and shaggy
the drovers like bears enduring untamed

Yet gentle with cattle watched over by night
in open stance found with shelter and water
the way prepared not too narrow or steep
ford on the river or swimmable deep

When herded on boats there were floors of heather
when swimming the kyle they were roped together
tail to head and rowers coursing the current

The drovers dealers cunning campaigners
gathered their tributes like streams from the hills
from each strath and glen the islands and coasts
cattle assembled shod and protected
to market at Falkirk or tryst at Crieff

Ten miles a day for twenty-eight days
rested and guarded each detail well noted
avoidance of tolls deterrence of raiders
to seek good grazing replenish supplies

When the cattle were sold
the drovers found work on lowland farms
and they sent the dogs home

Steadily pacing
through mountain and stream
moorland and gully
instinctively guided

The dogs would be recognised
welcomed and fed
at the changehouse or inn
they had graced coming south

How loved and known was this land of ours
the tracks made by use trailed by drovers and dogs
by ponies and cattle with flowers and foxes
plover and eagle through raiks and forests

How loved and known each season and weather
the land of the leal the world of the drover

Arrows of Love

We stand for Truth against the world
as Druids claim in northern lands
stone circles, sun and moon
trees, rivers, water, light
and deathly dark of winter's tomb

Pilgrim saints walked through the glens
their followers and scholars taught
communities of knowledge, shared,
passed on to weave the sacred lines
where measurement is wisdom carved

What is Truth? He made no sign
or did he somehow breathe 'I am'?
Brighter than the brightest star
prophet of the destined way
bearer of resurgent life

On earth and mountain, over sea
by whirlpool and promontory
where sands are white and orchids bloom
dragonflies will catch the sun
larks will singing claim the sky

One went to seek his wife
like Orpheus, in elegiac land
among the bells, the blue flowers,
arrows of love, arrows of death,
the pierced heart, the true 'I am'

On earth and mountain, over sea
pilgrim saints walked through the glens
we stand for truth against the world
the pierced heart, the true 'I am'
brighter than the brightest star

Dragons of climate change

Fled the dragon black of chaos
War and wasting, plague and famine
Turned the year back from darkness
Midwinter gloom and desperation
Withering of beast and human:
Now the pendulum has swung
Earth can turn towards compassion
Now the hero's triumph won

Time to lift the roof of sky
To free the earth from our oppression
Time to set the maiden free
To open up the sun's fruition
Bringing light of warmth and vision:
Time for plenitude and laughter
All that's dark is in remission
Longest day and full midsummer

Other dragons are approaching
Ocean floods devour the land
Tsunami tides devastating
Houses fields and all around
How can such a power be bound?
From behind the dragon's teeth
The hero's weapons will be found
The sacrificial victim safe

Dragon red of fire and drought
Burns and shrivels all that grows
Animals and plants are caught
In the desert wind that blows
Only vultures thrive and crows:
Who will bring the snow and rain
Till the river runs and flows?
The god of mountain and of plain

These four dragons now arisen
All together they attack
Not one by one but in succession
Chaos, flood, drought and black
Volcano and earthquake
Earth so dear to us, our home
Now the hero's hour has struck
Our time now to overcome

... Merlin in your crystal cave
Deep in the diamond of the day...
Edwin Muir

Merlin of Drumelzier
never trapped in history
return, as you have before
within your homely courtesy
tread our country, touch our shore
re-call us to our destiny

Merlin dwell among us now –
in whom will you be manifest?
What astral joining, axial shift
will crack the mirror, mend the rift
re-align above below
restore the balance, free the flow
fuse the spirits east and west?

Seven hundred years, a *trine*
a moment in the life of rocks
the perfectly-formed crystal
oxygen trapped with silicon
the shaft, the ray, the laser
strings, wings
omnia in the particle
light points, rainbow specks

Encompass in your field of vision
the nought that is, the airy nothing
invented or discovered pattern
ancient love made modern
courage for the future spiral
digital, virtual
assuage the yearning

Michael Scott, Thomas the Rhymer
Queen of Faery, Earth Mother
braid-weaver, story-teller
Donald, Gordon, Isabel Pagan
Nan Shepherd and Morelle
motley followers of the Grail

Woodman, healer, commonweal,
singer, musician, techno-skilled,
connect us on our quest.
Glad-giver, you will reveal
our next magician

Each word, each vision
each note, each chanson
each new discovery
virtuous visual elision
embrace our sphere, your love-soaked way

Merlin in your crystal cave
Deep in the diamond of the day

this stately whispering tree for me
and the wind and the sun, now here, now gone

MADE IN EDINBURGH

Luath Press Limited
committed to publishing well written books worth reading

LUATH PRESS takes its name from Robert Burns, whose little collie Luath (*Gael.*, swift or nimble) tripped up Jean Armour at a wedding and gave him the chance to speak to the woman who was to be his wife and the abiding love of his life. Burns called one of 'The Twa Dogs' Luath after Cuchullin's hunting dog in Ossian's *Fingal*. Luath Press was established in 1981 in the heart of Burns country, and now resides a few steps up the road from Burns' first lodgings on Edinburgh's Royal Mile. Luath offers you distinctive writing with a hint of unexpected pleasures.

Most bookshops in the UK, the US, Canada, Australia, New Zealand and parts of Europe either carry our books in stock or can order them for you. To order direct from us, please send a £sterling cheque, postal order, international money order or your credit card details (number, address of cardholder and expiry date) to us at the address below. Please add post and packing as follows: UK – £1.00 per delivery address; overseas surface mail – £2.50 per delivery address; overseas airmail – £3.50 for the first book to each delivery address, plus £1.00 for each additional book by airmail to the same address. If your order is a gift, we will happily enclose your card or message at no extra charge.

Luath Press Limited
543/2 Castlehill
The Royal Mile
Edinburgh EH1 2ND
Scotland
Telephone: 0131 225 4326 (24 hours)
Fax: 0131 225 4324
email: sales@luath.co.uk
Website: www.luath.co.uk